THE OCEANIC WHITETIP SHARK

By Sara Green

BELLWETHER MEDIA · MINNEAPOLIS, MN

Jump into the cockpit and take flight with Pilot books. Your journey will take you on high-energy adventures as you learn about all that is wild, weird, fascinating, and fun!

This edition first published in 2013 by Bellwether Media, Inc.

No part of this publication may be reproduced in whole or in part without written permission of the publisher. For information regarding permission, write to Bellwether Media, Inc., Attention: Permissions Department, 5357 Penn Avenue South, Minneapolis, MN 55419.

Library of Congress Cataloging-in-Publication Data

Green, Sara, 1964-
The oceanic whitetip shark / by Sara Green.
    p. cm. – (Pilot books: shark fact files)
Includes bibliographical references and index.
 Summary: "Engaging images accompany information about the oceanic whitetip shark. The combination of high-interest subject matter and narrative text is intended for students in grades 3 through 7"–Provided by publisher.
 ISBN 978-1-60014-805-7 (hardcover : alk. paper)
 1. Oceanic whitetip shark–Juvenile literature. I. Title.
 QL638.95.C3G745 2013
 597.3072'3–dc23
                    2012004407

Printed in the United States of America, North Mankato, MN.

TABLE OF CONTENTS

OCEANIC WHITETIP SHARK IDENTIFIED

A shark glides slowly through the ocean in search of prey. Its large **pectoral fins** and rounded **dorsal fin** have white tips. This is the oceanic whitetip shark, one of the most dangerous sharks in the world.

The oceanic whitetip sticks its short, blunt snout out of the water and sniffs the air. It catches the scent of a dead whale, one of its favorite meals. It drops back into the water and races other sharks to the feast!

The oceanic whitetip shark has a brownish gray back and a white belly. This **countershading** helps the whitetip sneak up on prey without being seen. The shark's round eyes have **nictitating membranes**. When the whitetip attacks, these close to protect the eyes from injury. Broad scales called **dermal denticles** cover the whitetip's body. They lie flat and are smooth to the touch.

human

oceanic whitetip shark

An adult whitetip is usually around 7 feet (2 meters) long, but it can grow to be as long as 13 feet (4 meters). Females are often slightly longer than males. Both males and females can weigh up to 370 pounds (168 kilograms).

OCEANIC WHITETIP SHARK
TRACKED

Whitetips are found in tropical and **temperate** waters all over the world. They prefer the open ocean far from land. They are often found at the surface, but they can swim to depths greater than 500 feet (150 meters). Whitetips sometimes hunt for prey in shallow waters near islands or over **continental shelves**.

= oceanic whitetip territory

N
W E
S

SMILE!

Scientists often use photography to track whitetip migration. They take photos of whitetips in their natural habitats and identify them by their unique marks.

Whitetips **migrate** when the water temperature changes. When it gets cooler, the sharks move to warmer waters. Males and females sometimes migrate in separate groups.

young oceanic whitetip shark

Whitetips are **viviparous**. Pups develop inside their mother for almost a year. Then the mother gives birth to a litter of 1 to 15 pups. Larger females often have larger litters.

At birth, the pups are around 25 inches (64 centimeters) long. They have black or tan fin tips. As they grow, the tips get lighter in color and eventually become white. Whitetips **mature** at 6 or 7 years old. At this time, they are around 6 feet (1.8 meters) long and still growing.

Whitetips hunt both day and night. They feed mainly on squid and fish, but they also eat sea turtles, birds, and dead whales. Whitetips have powerful jaws and sharp teeth. The upper teeth have a triangular shape and **serrated** edges. They easily cut through skin and bones. The lower teeth are serrated only at the tip. They are used to hold prey. Whitetips do not chew their food. They rip prey into bite-size chunks and swallow them whole.

FEEDING FRENZIES

A dead whale or large school of fish can send whitetips into a feeding frenzy. The sharks bite anything that moves, even other sharks!

Whitetips use highly developed senses to find prey. They rely mostly on their keen sense of smell. They often lift their snouts out of the water to sniff the air. This helps them locate surface prey that may be far away.

Whitetips can sense the **electric fields** of animals that live in the ocean. Small holes in their snouts called **ampullae of Lorenzini** detect these fields. Whitetips also have sensors called **lateral lines**. These run along the sides of their bodies. They allow sharks to feel movements made by prey. Whitetips also have a sharp sense of hearing. They can hear the sounds of ocean animals from miles away!

Pilot fish often swim with whitetips. The sharks protect pilot fish from other predators and provide leftover food. In return, pilot fish swim into the mouths of whitetips and clean their teeth. They also eat **parasites** that live on the sharks' skin.

Whitetips are also known to follow pilot whales. Some scientists believe this is because pilot whales are skilled at finding squid. When the whales dive for them, the whitetips follow close behind.

pilot whales

pilot fish

BOAT'S BEST FRIEND

Sailors used to call sharks "sea dogs" because of their habit of following ships. The oceanic whitetip is best known for this behavior.

OCEANIC WHITETIP SHARK

CURRENT STATUS

The population of the oceanic whitetip is in decline. Scientists believe the number of whitetips in the Atlantic Ocean dropped by over half between 1992 and 2000. **Overfishing** and certain fishing practices pose the greatest threats to whitetips. People hunt them for their meat, fins, and skin. The fins are used in shark fin soup, and the skin is made into leather.

Whitetips and other sharks are often caught as **bycatch** in nets and on fishing lines meant for other fish. Some fishers safely release the whitetips back into the sea, but others kill them for their fins. The International Union for Conservation of Nature (IUCN) lists the oceanic whitetip as **vulnerable**.

SHARK BRIEF

Common Name: Oceanic Whitetip Shark

Also Known As: Whitetip

Nickname: Sea Dog

Claim to Fame: Attacks on shipwreck victims

Hot Spots: Far from land in the Atlantic, Pacific, and Indian Oceans

Life Span: Up to 22 years

Current Status: Vulnerable (IUCN)

EXTINCT

EXTINCT IN THE WILD

CRITICALLY ENDANGERED

ENDANGERED

VULNERABLE

NEAR THREATENED

LEAST CONCERN

Today, people around the world are working to protect oceanic whitetip sharks. Many fishers have stopped using bait that attracts whitetips. The United States and some other countries have banned **finning**.

Whitetips play an important role in the oceans of the world. They help keep the waters clean by eating sick or weak prey. They also help prevent prey populations from growing too large. As more steps are taken to protect oceanic whitetips, the sharks can reclaim their reign of the open sea.

GLOSSARY

ampullae of Lorenzini—a network of tiny jelly-filled sacs around a shark's snout; the jelly is sensitive to the electric fields of nearby prey.

bycatch—animals that are accidentally caught with fishing nets or lines

continental shelves—flat, underwater extensions of a continent that drop to the ocean floor

countershading—coloring that helps camouflage an animal; fish with countershading have pale bellies and dark backs.

dermal denticles—small, tooth-like scales that cover some types of fish

dorsal fin—a fin on the back of a fish

electric fields—waves of electricity created by movement; every living being has an electric field.

finning—the practice of cutting off a shark's fins at sea and tossing the shark back into the water

lateral lines—a system of tubes beneath a shark's skin that helps it detect changes in water pressure

mature—to become able to reproduce

migrate—to move from one place to another, often with the seasons

nictitating membranes—whitish inner eyelids that close to protect a shark's eyes when it attacks prey

overfishing—greatly reducing the number of fish in an area by fishing too much

parasites—organisms that live off of other organisms

pectoral fins—a pair of fins that extend from each side of a fish's body

serrated—having a jagged edge

temperate—neither too warm nor too cold

viviparous—producing young that develop inside the body; viviparous animals give birth to live young.

vulnerable—at risk of becoming endangered

TO LEARN MORE

At the Library

Berman, Ruth. *Sharks*. Minneapolis, Minn.: Lerner Publications, 2009.

Musgrave, Ruth. *National Geographic Kids Everything Sharks*. Washington, D.C.: National Geographic, 2011.

Van Briesen, Shawn. *Discovery Channel Top 10 Deadliest Sharks*. Horsham, Pa.: Zenescope Entertainment, 2010.

On the Web

Learning more about oceanic whitetip sharks is as easy as 1, 2, 3.

1. Go to www.factsurfer.com.

2. Enter "oceanic whitetip sharks" into the search box.

3. Click the "Surf" button and you will see a list of related Web sites.

With factsurfer.com, finding more information is just a click away.

INDEX